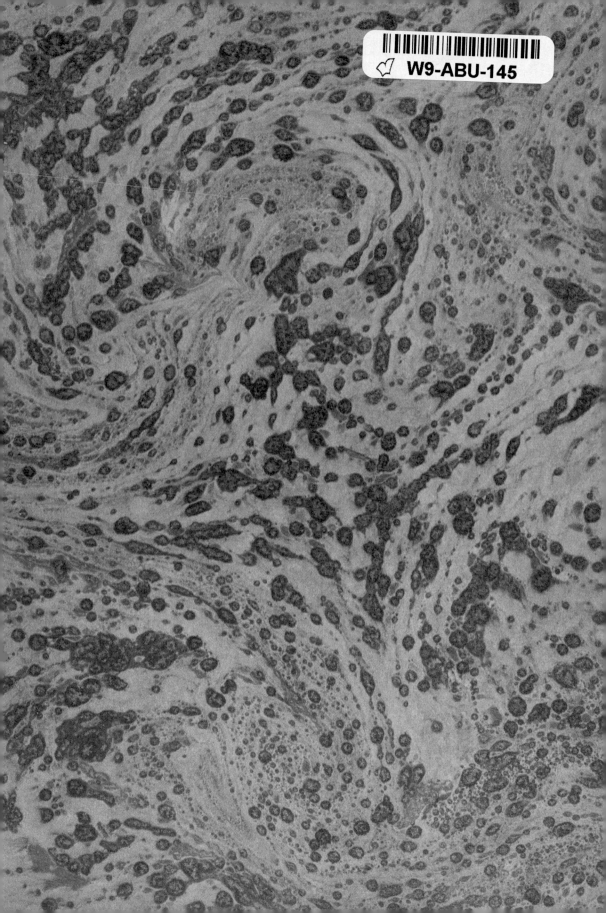

Be You

"The Lord has sent you down to earth
If some one else could serve His plan
There'd be no reason for your birth,
He would have sent another man
But for some purpose kept from view
We must believe He wanted you."

Edgar Guest

ENGLISH PAINTING

by

M. Le Frere Carroll

&

Frances Cavanah

(National Portrait Gallery, London)

Sir Joshua Reynolds   *Self-Portrait*

Grosset & Dunlap

Publishers   New York

WILLIAM HOGARTH, *The Shrimp Girl*

(National Gallery, London)

JOHN CONSTABLE, *Salisbury Cathedral from the Meadows*

ENGLISH PAINTING

England seems to have been the Rip Van Winkle of the art world. For several centuries she was apparently unstirred by any artistic urge such as motivated other European countries. Because of political and religious strife, there was no great Church Art, and it was not until the sixteenth century, when Henry VII decided to have his portrait done, that there was any real interest in painting. Henry thought he might increase his popularity by sending a likeness of himself to every province within the kingdom. Because native artists were unequal to the task, he had to call in Italian artists, and portraiture soon became the vogue in England.

For many years after that English art was dominated by outsiders. The German portraitist, Hans Holbein the Younger, was a favorite with Henry VIII. After Charles I came to the throne in 1625, he called to the Court the great Flemish master, Anthony Van Dyck, who influenced English painters for years to come. Though he had some native pupils, the men who did the most to carry on his tradition were foreigners like Sir Peter Lely (1618-1680), a Dutch painter who had settled in London.

(See Lely's portrait, *Lady Byron,* Plate IV.) Thus it happened that portraiture, one of the great achievements of English art, was given its first impetus by outsiders.

It was not until the time of William Hogarth (1697-1764) that England produced an outstanding artist who had been born on English soil. He started his career as an engraver, but he never forgot his desire to be a painter. He was always the pioneer. In his *Shrimp Girl* (Plate I), for instance, there is a remarkable departure from the finished technique of his day. It has instead the free, sketchy manner later used by the impressionists of the nineteenth century. But portrait painting did not come easily to Hogarth. He was too truthful, and the truth did not always sit well with his fashionable models. To meet expenses, he turned to painting small conversation pieces, so called because they showed dramatic little scenes from life. Though he himself belittled them, some of them—for instance, *The Wedding of Mr. Stephen Beckingham* (Plate VII)—have a beauty of line and color not usually found in his work.

What really interested Hogarth were pictures reflecting the life and customs of his day, pictures that pointed a moral. He painted them in series, working towards a climax, very much as a dramatist arranges the scenes in a play. *Morning* (Plate VIII) was one of a series called TIMES OF THE DAY. *The Rake's Levee* (Plate V) was one of eight pictures called RAKE'S PROGRESS which showed the adventures and downfall of a gay young spendthrift. In order to reach the general public with his preachments, Hogarth had engravings made and sold the prints. The subjects were often unpleasant and could scarcely be called works of art, but because of their biting satire, once seen they were not easily forgotten. This was equally true of his caricatures. (See Plate III.)

(Pl. III) WILLIAM HOGARTH, *The Sawsetter*

It is hard to imagine a man more unlike Hogarth than his successor,

4

(Pl. IV) SIR PETER LELY, *Lady Byron*

Sir Joshua Reynolds (1723-1792). Yet Sir Joshua learned a great deal from Hogarth. For that matter, though, he learned from every artist whose works he ever studied. "His materials were generally borrowed, but the noble structure was his own," he once said of Raphael, but he might have said it of himself with equal truth.

Sir Joshua had an uncanny ability of posing his sitters in natural, life-

(Pl. V) WILLIAM HOGARTH, *The Rake's Levee,* from *The Rake's Progress*

like attitudes. And unlike any English artist who had gone before him, he provided his charming figures with charming landscape backgrounds. His coloring, his rendering of light and shadow were superb, and the result was such luminous and graceful canvasses as *Portrait of Mrs. Lloyds* (Plate VI). Sir Joshua usually painted the aristocrats in whose society he moved, not only women but men. (See *Sir Philip Ainslie,* Plate XII.) He also left some revealing *Self-Portraits.* (See title page.)

In whatever way one uses the term, Sir Joshua was one of the most successful men who ever lived. He had many friends, including the most important people of his time. When the Royal Academy was founded, he was elected its first president. He was knighted by King George III. His lectures and discourses on art won wide recognition. He painted about 3000 pictures, painted them so brilliantly and so rapidly that he found more time than the average artist for the gay round of social activities in eighteenth century London. Even the handicap of deafness— and toward the end of his life, blindness—could not disturb his serene and cheerful disposition.

Yet Sir Joshua did have an occasional pang of jealousy. So dynamic

6

(Collection of Baron Rothschild)

(Pl. VI) Sir Joshua Reynolds, *Portrait of Mrs. Lloyds*

(Pl. VII) WILLIAM HOGARTH, *The Wedding of Stephen Beckingham*

a man was bound to have rivals, none of whom caused him more alarm than Thomas Gainsborough (1727-1788). Gainsborough never knew how to draw a figure correctly, nor were his compositions so well balanced as those of his rival. But for the sheer poetry and charm he had no equal among his contemporaries. For Reynolds' study of the old masters, he substituted the study of nature. A friendly sort of man, he was none the less quick-tempered and easily provoked by dogmatic statements. When Reynolds said in a lecture before the Academy that no work of art could be produced without a balance of cold and warm colors, Gainsborough resolved to paint a masterpiece, in which only cold colors were used. The result was *The Blue Boy,* one of the best known pictures in the world.

Perhaps the main reason Gainsborough lagged behind Reynolds as a portrait painter lay in his disposition. The social demands of portrait painting irked him. On one occasion a conceited noble in a rich new suit of clothes and a powdered wig came to sit for him, with the request, "Now, sir, I beg you will not overlook the dimple on my chin." Gainsborough, already exasperated by the artificial pose his model had assumed, threw down his brushes in disgust. "Confound the dimple on your chin. I shall neither paint the one nor the other."

It was small wonder therefore that Gainsborough, who always preferred his native Suffolk to London, should have found his greatest pleasure in landscape painting. He never forgot that nature had been his first teacher. He was especially successful in combining his figures with a landscape background, as in *Promenade in the Morning* (Plate X).

The third fashionable painter of the eighteenth century was George Romney (1734-1802). He, even more than Gainsborough, incurred the dislike of Reynolds, who saw to it that Romney was not admitted to the Royal Academy. "Romney and Reynolds divide the town," said one of their contemporaries, for all London seemed to take sides in the controversy between the two artists. Romney's studio was thronged by fashionable people. His canvasses had a gayety and warmth, a feeling for color, and an elegance that pleased an elegant society.

The portrait of *William Pitt as a Boy* (Plate XIV) shows Romney's success with pictures of children. His *Mother and Child* (Plate XIII) is one of the

(*Courtesy of* The Metropolitan Museum of Art)
(Pl. VIII) WILLIAM HOGARTH, *Morning,* from *Times of the Day*

9

(Pl. IX) Thomas Gainsborough, *Cottage in the Woods*

most tender expressions of maternal love ever painted.

After Reynolds' death, his successor as president of the Royal Academy was Benjamin West (1738-1820). Though an American, West chose to work as an English painter. His best known pictures depict events from the history of his time. Among them were *The Death of General Wolfe* and *Penn's Treaty with the Indians*.

In contrast, his younger contemporary, William Blake (1757-1827), has been called a painter of dreams. But Blake was too intangible to be popular. Today we remember him as a poet, rather than an artist, especially for his exquisite *Songs of Innocence*.

One of the best liked artists of his day was Thomas Rowlandson (1756-1827), whose work recalls the satire of Hogarth. A large, burly, good-natured fellow, during his travels in France he was mistaken by many an innkeeper's wife for John Bull, that mythical personage of whom they had so often heard. Rowlandson's accomplishments at the table and at the easel were said to have been equally remarkable. Perhaps no artist ever painted more easily. Some of his portraits of women are so lovely that they have been mistaken for the work of Gainsborough, but he was equally adept at showing the life of London's poor. He might easily have

(Pl. X) Thomas Gainsborough, *Promenade in the Morning*

(Pl. XI) THOMAS GAINSBOROUGH, *The Market Cart*

ranked with Sir Joshua, according to Sir Joshua himself.

However, like so many people with a superabundance of talent, Rowlandson too often frittered his away, content to paint frivolous pictures that would bring him quick popularity.

Another artist that pleased Sir Joshua was Henry Raeburn (1756-1823), who was later to prefix a "Sir" to his own name. Though he had

(Pl. XII) SIR JOSHUA REYNOLDS, *Sir Philip Ainslie*

(Pl. XIII) George Romney, *Mother and Child*

had some study in his native Scotland, he had practically taught himself to paint. Orders came pouring in, but though financially secure, he had the good sense to realize that he could never do the great things of which he was capable without further study. On the advice of Sir Joshua he spent two years in Rome, then returned to Edinburgh an even finer artist.

Most of the city's distinguished men sat for Raeburn, and every schoolboy knows his portrait of *Sir Walter Scott*. His portrait of *Sir John Clerke and Lady Clerke* (Plate XVIII) shows the soft, suffused light for which his work was noted. He was an intuitive artist. Before a first sitting was over, he had usually made up his mind about the personality of his model and was able to reveal it with ease and clarity.

In contrast to Sir Henry was his contemporary, John Hoppner (1758-1810) of whom it was said, "In his constant wish to represent the gentleman, he sometimes failed to delineate the man." However, some of his portraits do show character, and they had a great richness of color. As a popular painter he had only one serious rival in his own time.

That rival was Sir Thomas Lawrence (1769-1830), as charming a gentleman as Hoppner himself and one just as clever at flattering his sitters. The rivalry that sprang up between the two men was as keen as that which had once existed between Reynolds and Romney. In the end Lawrence's fascinating style won him the victory.

Lawrence, a child prodigy, opened a studio in the fashionable town of Bath when he was only twelve. Here flocked the eminent men and the beautiful women of the day, all eager to sit for the gay artist. By the time he was eighteen he had established himself in London. At the insistence of George III, he was admitted to the Royal Academy when he was twenty-two, several years under the usual age required for member-

(Pl. XIV) GEORGE ROMNEY, *William Pitt as a Boy*

(Pl. XV) Sir Thomas Lawrence, *A Child with a Kid*

(Pl. XVI) Sir Thomas Lawrence, *Nature*

ship. He painted some of his best pictures before he was twenty-five.

Lawrence's weakness was that he was too eager for fame. Too often he sacrificed quality to quantity, he resorted to tricks of line and color which hardly stand the test of artistic scrutiny. But he did have the great virtue of originality. Instead of imitating the old Italian and Flemish masters, he expressed the age in which he lived. It was an artificial age, but the people he painted seemed alive and he knew how to catch the most subtle expression on a face. His most appealing pictures were those of children. Among them were *A Child with a Kid* (Plate XV) and *Nature* (Plate XVI).

Lawrence exerted a decided influence on his fellow painters, an influence not always to the good. There was John Opie (1761-1807), for in-

(Pl. XVII) J. M. W. Turner, *The Blacksmith Shop*

stance, who started his career as a painter of simple folk. Had he only remained in his native Cornwall, he might have gone down in history as one of the mighty. Instead, he was discovered by Peter Pindar, famous English satirist, taken to London, introduced to fashionable society, and besieged with orders for portraits. Here, he tried to imitate the brilliant and surface effects of Lawrence, and as a result, his style became faltering, where it had once been direct.

But fortunately, the fickle society of London soon tired of "the Cornish wonder" with his rough, unpolished manners. Opie, who had been largely self-taught, began a serious study of the technique of his art, and his natural vigor had a chance to assert itself. A few years later he painted the historical pictures that won him election to the Academy. But his best work was in portraits.

By the end of the eighteenth century English painting was recognized in Europe for its distinctive style. It combined some of the best attributes of the Dutch, Flemish and Italian masters and to these added a sensitive quality of color and atmosphere not shared by any other school of painting. English artists had made a solid contribution to art in the field of portraiture. But beginning with the work of Gainsborough and Richard Wilson (1714-1782), they made what was perhaps an even greater contribution to landscape painting.

Wilson has been called "the father of English landscape," but it is a

(Pl. XVIII) Sir Henry Raeburn, *Sir John Clerke and Lady Clerke*

question whether the title rightfully belongs to him or to Gainsborough. Starting his career as a portrait painter, Wilson visited Italy where he came under the influence of Claude Lorrain and the old mythology. When he returned, he began to inject bits of Italian scenery into his paintings.

Gainsborough went a step farther by concentrating on the rustic settings so typical of his own Suffolk. His pictures were much more to the average Englishman's taste, for in them he could see reflected the native land he loved so well. In such paintings as *Cottage in the Woods* (Plate IX) and *The Market Cart* (Plate XI), Gainsborough was at his best. He never left England. He did not need to, for to him the scenes of his own countryside were more beautiful than those any foreign land could offer.

With John Crome (1768-1821), a native of Norwich, began the effort to make a landscape an exact portrait of a definite scene. The old Dutch masters of landscape—Hobbema, Ruysdael, and Cuyp—were his inspiration, yet he remained distinctly English. In his later years, "Old Crome," as he came to be known, organized the Norwich School of Landscape, which gave a new zest to the nature movement.

Up to this time English painters had been using oils almost exclusively. Water color had been used merely to paint trifling details, until artists discovered that this medium enabled them to paint more rapidly and with more spontaneity. The idea proved so popular that it soon spread all over the art world. The great master of water color, in the opinion of some

(Victoria and Albert Museum, London)

(Pl. XIX) JOHN CROME, *Mousehold Heath*

(Pl. XX) JOHN CONSTABLE, *Portrait of Mrs. Pulham*

critics the greatest who ever lived, was J. M. W. Turner (1775-1851). His color, though often unnatural, was none the less wonderful. He was a dreamer, and he transmitted his dreams to canvas in colors as glowing as those Titian might have used.

Like Richard Wilson, Turner turned to the great French landscapist Claude Lorrain, for inspiration. However, he had an eye for striking and sensational effects, and he did not limit himself to literary and historical pictures. He was just as likely to seize upon a modern subject if it proved glamorous. Such widely different subjects as *The Blacksmith Shop* (Plate XVII) and *Dido Building, Carthage* took form under his facile brush.

Turner was always experimenting and the results were naturally uneven. But, as one critic said, "His artistic nature, with all its errors, was one of the most opulent that ever existed." His personality was just as unpredictable as his work. Though accused of having a miserly, jealous disposition, he was capable of the most generous gestures toward his fellow artists. At one exhibition in London the bright colors of his picture called *Cologne* tended to show up to a disadvantage two portraits by Sir Thomas Lawrence that hung on either side. So Turner voluntarily ruined the effect of his beautiful goldine sky by painting over it with lamp black. "Oh, poor Lawrence was so unhappy," he said. "It'll all wash off after the exhibition."

The charge was true that Turner was a miser. If his patrons hesitated too long over the price of a picture, he put the price up while they hesitated. Yet much as he loved money, it was almost more than he could bear to part with a painting. For days after a sale he would wear a martyred expression, explaining to his friends, "I've lost one of my children this week."

It would be hard to find a more striking contrast to Turner than his contemporary, John Constable (1776-1837). Both painted landscape, but with what a difference! Whereas Turner painted visions—"golden visions" they have been called—Constable was once known to remark, "Thank Heaven, I have no imagination!"

Constable aspired to be "a natural painter." As a boy of sixteen he had been a miller, and that year, watching the clouds sweep across the sky, did more to set the mold of his career than the formal art training that came later. He had no other wish than to paint the simple, rural scenes of his native Suffolk, and to paint them directly from nature. He stuck to his purpose through the years, and when at the age of forty-eight his *Hay Wain* (Plate XXI) was exhibited at the Paris Salon, it changed the entire trend of French landscape painting.

The Hay Wain is a pleasant enough picture, but today it is hard to understand why it should have caused such a sensation. For many years now it has been a common enough thing to paint directly from nature, but then it was a novelty. Constable had said of his contemporaries, "They study pictures only." *The Hay Wain* was the beginning of a reaction against the slavish imitation of classical masters.

Constable also painted portraits (see the portrait, *Mrs. Pulham,* Plate XX), but he did it only to make money. We remember him chiefly for his peaceful views of England. His finest work—the picture he himself liked best—was *Salisbury Cathedral from the Meadows* (Plate II).

Constable and Turner had only one serious rival in their own day. That was Richard Parkes Bonington (1801-1828), who might possibly

(Pl. XXI) John Constable, *The Hay Wain*

(Pl. XXII) FREDERICK WATTS, *The Old Bridge*

have become even more famous than they, had he not died at twenty-six. He spent most of his short life in France, painting such brilliant little masterpieces as *A Park of Versailles* (Plate XXVI). Though he also worked in oils, it is for his watercolors we best remember him.

In 1822 John Constable prophesied, "The art will go out. There will be no genuine painting in England in thirty years." In 1852 it looked as though his gloomy words had indeed come true. The pictures being produced were very trivial, though the artists slavishly followed the hidebound rules laid down by Sir Joshua Reynolds. He had formulated these rules after a careful study of Raphael, whom he considered the supreme painter by whose standards all other painters should be judged.

At last, though, there arose a young artist, Holman Hunt (1827-1910), who believed that Sir Joshua had substituted a false standard of grace and beauty for a study of nature. Rather should modern artists look to those great primitives who had preceded Raphael and try to recapture something of their originality and simplicity. Together with two friends, John Millais and Dante Rossetti, Hunt founded the pre-Raphaelite Brotherhood, made up of very earnest young men, both artists and poets.

Fortunately, the Brotherhood had courage. They were laughed at, lied about, viciously attacked by the press. Older artists and critics were shocked that they should have dared defy the conventions of established painting. Finally John Ruskin, noted writer and critic, came forward as their champion, declaring that they were laying "the foundation of a school of art nobler than the world has seen for 300 years."

What the Brotherhood accomplished was to make English art less smug. Though there were some remarkable members, they were never wholly successful as a group. In their effort to copy the Italian primitives and to render nature faithfully, they too often clogged their work with details that ruined their efforts as a whole. Holman Hunt, the founder, was always a preacher rather than an artist.

In contrast to Hunt with his very labored pictures was Dante Gabriel Rossetti (1828-1882) with his great fund of natural talent. He came of an Italian family and was noted as much as a poet as an artist. When he joined the Brotherhood he shared Hunt's religious fervor, but gradually he formed his own philosophy. *The Daydream* (Plate XXIII) is one of his loveliest pictures.

(Victoria and Albert Museum, London)

(Pl. XXIII) Dante Rossetti, *The Day Dream*

Strangely enough, Rossetti, who came to believe that true art should be without any practical purpose, finally turned his talents to designing furniture. He joined forces with William Morris, " the poet upholsterer," who revolted against the ugly, ornate household furnishings of his time and opened his own factory. Here furniture of beautiful, simple lines was made, as well as colored rugs and tapestries and stained glass windows. It was the beginning of an artistic revolution in England, which helped to bring to an end the ugly ostentation of the Victorian era.

The greatest of the pre-Raphaelites was John Millais (1829-1896). Even as a child, he seemed destined for success. On one occasion when

(Pl. XXIV) John Millais, *Death of Ophelia*

the Society of Arts conducted a competition, the name of "Mr. Millais" was called out as the winner. Then to everyone's surprise a nine-year-old boy came forward to claim the silver medal. By the time he was nineteen he was already famous.

Yet he did not hesitate to risk his popularity by joining forces with Rossetti and Hunt. With them he set out on a romantic quest for that natural beauty which he believed most clearly expressed in the work of the Italian primitives. He was never as ardent a pre-Raphaelite as his two friends. But his technical skill was greater than theirs, and he did more than any one person to make the movement popular.

During the ten years that Millais was a member of the Brotherhood, he did some of his best work. His *Death of Ophelia* (Plate XXIV) is one of the great pictures in English art. In this he has rendered the foliage and flowers so accurately that even botanists have approved. Yet he has not detracted from the lovely effect as a whole, as so often happened in the work of his fellow artists.

One of the famous disciples of the Brotherhood was Sir Edward Burne-Jones (1833-1898). He never even saw a good picture until he was twenty-three, but at Oxford where he went to study for the ministry he fell under the spell of the old Greek and Latin poets. Here also he met William Morris, and in reading *Morte d'Arthur,* the two youths found refuge from the ugliness of the present in the beauty of the past. After Burne-Jones saw

(Pl. XXV) Sir Edward Burne-Jones, *Circe*

his first picture by Rossetti he knew that he also wished to be a painter. Rather later than most students, he settled down in London to learn the rudiments of drawing. Both Rossetti and Ruskin, realizing he had genius, befriended him, bought his pictures, advised him to go to Rome to study.

Circe (Plate XXV) is a typical Burne-Jones picture. He was a highly imaginative painter, who turned to the past for his subjects. But his love of beauty found expression in many forms. He had a highly developed decorative sense, and he designed exquisite stained glass windows. He also joined the firm of William Morris, furnishing designs for tapestry and needle-work, bas-reliefs and titles, and illustrated some of Morris's books.

Two artists with a leaning toward the pre-Raphaelites, yet remaining apart from them, were George Frederick Watts and Ford Madox Brown. Brown (1821-1893) was an idealist with strong religious convictions. *Christ Washing Peter's Feet* is one of the best known of his works.

We most frequently associate the name of George Frederick Watts (1817-1904) with such popular pictures as *Hope* and *Sir Galahad*. He himself said, "My intention has not been so much to paint pictures that will charm the eye as to suggest great thoughts . . . "

Watts' choice of subjects was wide. It included landscapes (See *The Old Bridge,* Plate XXII) and scenes from classic legends. But his greatest achievement was as a portrait painter. He asked many eminent men to sit for him, among them Tennyson, Browning, Carlyle, Gladstone and Matthew Arnold, so that he might make England a gift of the portraits of the great men of the times. They are now in the National Gallery in London.

There have been many other good English artists, of course, among them John Crome (1741-1801), a distinguished engraver of landscapes (See *Mousehold Heath: Boy Keeping Sheep,* Plate XIX); Sir David Wilkie (1785-1841) who was at his best as a painter of village people and their simple festivities; and Sir Edwin Landseer (1802-1873), whose animal pictures are known to every child. But English art had reached its greatest glory during the eighteenth century, in the work, so many people believe, of John Constable. Since his influence was destined to survive him and to extend to other lands, it has remained a potent force in the world of art.

(Pl. XXVI) RICHARD BONINGTON, *A Park of Versailles*

28